THE WHITE HOUSE

WASHINGTON

Today, the United States is stronger and better positioned to seize the opportunities of a still new century and safeguard our interests against the risks of an insecure world.

America's growing economic strength is the foundation of our national security and a critical source of our influence abroad. Since the Great Recession, we have created nearly 11 million new jobs during the longest private sector job growth in our history. Unemployment has fallen to its lowest level in 6 years. We are now the world leader in oil and gas production. We continue to set the pace for science, technology, and innovation in the global economy.

We also benefit from a young and growing workforce, and a resilient and diversified economy. The entrepreneurial spirit of our workers and businesses undergirds our economic edge. Our higher education system is the finest in the world, drawing more of the best students globally every year. We continue to attract immigrants from every corner of the world who renew our country with their energy and entrepreneurial talents.

Globally, we have moved beyond the large ground wars in Iraq and Afghanistan that defined so much of American foreign policy over the past decade. Compared to the nearly 180,000 troops we had in Iraq and Afghanistan when I took office, we now have fewer than 15,000 deployed in those countries. We possess a military whose might, technology, and geostrategic reach is unrivaled in human history. We have renewed our alliances from Europe to Asia.

Now, at this pivotal moment, we continue to face serious challenges to our national security, even as we are working to shape the opportunities of tomorrow. Violent extremism and an evolving terrorist threat raise a persistent risk of attacks on America and our allies. Escalating challenges to cybersecurity, aggression by Russia, the accelerating impacts of climate change, and the outbreak of infectious diseases all give rise to anxieties about global security. We must be clear-eyed about these and other challenges and recognize the United States has a unique capability to mobilize and lead the international community to meet them.

Any successful strategy to ensure the safety of the American people and advance our national security interests must begin with an undeniable truth—America must lead. Strong and sustained American leadership is essential to a rules-based international order that promotes global security and prosperity as well as the dignity and human rights of all peoples. The question is never whether America should lead, but how we lead.

Abroad, we are demonstrating that while we will act unilaterally against threats to our core interests, we are stronger when we mobilize collective action. That is why we are leading international coalitions to confront the acute challenges posed by aggression, terrorism, and disease. We are leading over 60 partners in a global campaign to degrade and ultimately defeat the Islamic State of Iraq and the Levant (ISIL) in Iraq and Syria, including by working to disrupt the flow of foreign fighters to those countries, while keeping pressure on al-Qa'ida. We are leading a global effort to stop the deadly spread of the Ebola virus at its source. In lockstep with our European allies, we are enforcing tough sanctions on Russia to impose costs and deter future aggression.

Even as we meet these pressing challenges, we are pursuing historic opportunities. Our rebalance to Asia and the Pacific is yielding deeper ties with a more diverse set of allies and partners. When complete, the Trans-Pacific Partnership will generate trade and investment opportunities—and create high-quality jobs at home—across a region that represents more than 40 percent of global trade. We are primed to unlock the potential of our relationship with India. The scope of our cooperation with China is unprecedented, even as we remain alert to China's military modernization and reject any role for intimidation in resolving territorial disputes. We are deepening our investment in Africa, accelerating access to energy, health, and food security in a rapidly rising region. Our opening to Cuba will enhance our engagement in our own hemisphere, where there are enormous opportunities to consolidate gains in pursuit of peace, prosperity, democracy, and energy security.

Globally, we are committed to advancing the Prague Agenda, including by stopping the spread of nuclear weapons and securing nuclear materials. We are currently testing whether it is possible to achieve a comprehensive resolution to assure the international community that Iran's nuclear program is peaceful, while the Joint Plan of Action has halted the progress of Iran's program. We are building on our own energy security—and the ground-breaking commitment we made with China to reduce greenhouse gas emissions—to cement an international consensus on arresting climate change. We are shaping global standards for cybersecurity and building international capacity to disrupt and investigate cyber threats. We are playing a leading role in defining the international community's post-2015 agenda for eliminating extreme poverty and promoting sustainable development while prioritizing women and youth.

Underpinning it all, we are upholding our enduring commitment to the advancement of democracy and human rights and building new coalitions to combat corruption and to support open governments and open societies. In doing so, we are working to support democratic transitions, while also reaching out to the drivers of change in this century: young people and entrepreneurs.

Finally, I believe that America leads best when we draw upon our hopes rather than our fears. To succeed, we must draw upon the power of our example—that means viewing our commitment to our values and the rule of law as a strength, and not an inconvenience. That is why I have worked to ensure that America has the capabilities we need to respond to threats abroad, while acting in line with our values—prohibiting the use of torture; embracing constraints on our use of new technologies like drones; and upholding our commitment to privacy and civil liberties. These actions are a part of our resilience at home and a source of our influence abroad.

On all these fronts, America leads from a position of strength. But, this does not mean we can or should attempt to dictate the trajectory of all unfolding events around the world. As powerful as we are and will remain, our resources and influence are not infinite. And in a complex world, many of the security problems we face do not lend themselves to quick and easy fixes. The United States will always defend our interests and uphold our commitments to allies and partners. But, we have to make hard choices among many competing priorities, and we must always resist the over-reach that comes when we make decisions based upon fear. Moreover, we must recognize that a smart national security strategy does not rely solely on military power. Indeed, in the long-term, our efforts to work with other countries to counter the ideology and root causes of violent extremism will be more important than our capacity to remove terrorists from the battlefield.

The challenges we face require strategic patience and persistence. They require us to take our responsibilities seriously and make the smart investments in the foundations of our national power. Therefore, I will continue to pursue a comprehensive agenda that draws on all elements of our national strength, that is attuned to the strategic risks and opportunities we face, and that is guided by the principles and priorities set out in this strategy. Moreover, I will continue to insist on budgets that safeguard our strength and work with the Congress to end sequestration, which undercuts our national security.

This is an ambitious agenda, and not everything will be completed during my Presidency. But I believe this is an achievable agenda, especially if we proceed with confidence and if we restore the bipartisan center that has been a pillar of strength for American foreign policy in decades past. As Americans, we will always have our differences, but what unites us is the national consensus that American global leadership remains indispensable. We embrace our exceptional role and responsibilities at a time when our unique contributions and capabilities are needed most, and when the choices we make today can mean greater security and prosperity for our Nation for decades to come.

Table of Contents

I. Introduction 1

II. Security 7

    Strengthen Our National Defense 7

    Reinforce Homeland Security 8

    Combat the Persistent Threat of Terrorism 9

    Build Capacity to Prevent Conflict 10

    Prevent the Spread and Use of Weapons of Mass Destruction 11

    Confront Climate Change 12

    Assure Access to Shared Spaces 12

    Increase Global Health Security 13

III. Prosperity 15

    Put Our Economy to Work 15

    Advance Our Energy Security 16

    Lead in Science, Technology, and Innovation 16

    Shape the Global Economic Order 16

    End Extreme Poverty 17

IV. Values 19

    Live Our Values 19

    Advance Equality 20

    Support Emerging Democracies 20

    Empower Civil Society and Young Leaders 21

    Prevent Mass Atrocities 22

V. International Order 23

    Advance Our Rebalance to Asia and the Pacific 24

    Strengthen Our Enduring Alliance with Europe 25

    Seek Stability and Peace in the Middle East and North Africa 26

    Invest in Africa's Future 26

    Deepen Economic and Security Cooperation in the Americas 27

VI. Conclusion 29

I. Introduction

In a young century, opportunities for America abound, but risks to our security remain. This new *National Security Strategy* positions the United States to safeguard our national interests through strong and sustainable leadership. It sets out the principles and priorities to guide the use of American power and influence in the world. It advances a model of American leadership rooted in the foundation of America's economic and technological strength and the values of the American people. It redoubles our commitment to allies and partners and welcomes the constructive contributions of responsible rising powers. It signals our resolve and readiness to deter and, if necessary, defeat potential adversaries. It affirms America's leadership role within a rules-based international order that works best through empowered citizens, responsible states, and effective regional and international organizations. And it serves as a compass for how this Administration, in partnership with the Congress, will lead the world through a shifting security landscape toward a more durable peace and a new prosperity.

This strategy builds on the progress of the last 6 years, in which our active leadership has helped the world recover from a global economic crisis and respond to an array of emerging challenges. Our progress includes strengthening an unrivaled alliance system, underpinned by our enduring partnership with Europe, while investing in nascent multilateral forums like the G-20 and East Asia Summit. We brought most of our troops home after more than a decade of honorable service in two wars while adapting our counterterrorism strategy for an evolving terrorist threat. We led a multinational coalition to support the Afghan government to take responsibility for the security of their country, while supporting Afghanistan's first peaceful, democratic transition of power. The United States led the international response to natural disasters, including the earthquake in Haiti, the earthquake and tsunami in Japan, and the typhoon in the Philippines to save lives, prevent greater damage, and support efforts to rebuild. We led international efforts to stop the proliferation of nuclear weapons, including by building an unprecedented international sanctions regime to hold Iran responsible for failing to meet its international obligations, while pursuing a diplomatic effort that has already stopped the progress of Iran's nuclear program and rolled it back in key respects. We are rebalancing toward Asia and the Pacific while seeking new opportunities for partnership and investment in Africa and the Americas, where we have spurred greater agriculture and energy-related investments than ever before. And at home and abroad, we are taking concerted action to confront the dangers posed by climate change and to strengthen our energy security.

Still, there is no shortage of challenges that demand continued American leadership. The potential proliferation of weapons of mass destruction, particularly nuclear weapons, poses a grave risk. Even as we have decimated al-Qa'ida's core leadership, more diffuse networks of al-Qa'ida, ISIL, and affiliated groups threaten U.S. citizens, interests, allies, and partners. Violent extremists exploit upheaval across the Middle East and North Africa. Fragile and conflict-affected states incubate and spawn infectious disease, illicit weapons and drug smugglers, and destabilizing refugee flows. Too often, failures in governance and endemic corruption hold back the potential of rising regions. The danger of disruptive and even destructive cyber-attack is growing, and the risk of another global economic slowdown remains. The international community's ability to respond effectively to these and other risks is helped or hindered by the behaviors of major powers. Where progress has been most profound, it is due to the steadfastness of our allies and the cooperation of other emerging powers.

These complex times have made clear the power and centrality of America's indispensable leadership in the world. We mobilized and are leading global efforts to impose costs to counter Russian aggression, to degrade and ultimately defeat ISIL, to squelch the Ebola virus at its source, to stop the spread of nuclear weapons materials, and to turn the corner on global carbon emissions. A strong consensus endures across our political spectrum that the question is not *whether* America will lead, but *how* we will lead into the future.

First and foremost, we will **lead with purpose.** American leadership is a global force for good, but it is grounded in our enduring national interests as outlined in the 2010 *National Security Strategy*:

- The security of the United States, its citizens, and U.S. allies and partners;

- A strong, innovative, and growing U.S. economy in an open international economic system that promotes opportunity and prosperity;

- Respect for universal values at home and around the world; and

- A rules-based international order advanced by U.S. leadership that promotes peace, security, and opportunity through stronger cooperation to meet global challenges.

Especially in a changing global environment, these national interests will continue to guide all we do in the world. To advance these interests most effectively, we must pursue a comprehensive national security agenda, allocate resources accordingly, and work with the Congress to end sequestration. Even so, our resources will never be limitless. Policy tradeoffs and hard choices will need to be made. In such instances, we will prioritize efforts that address the top strategic risks to our interests:

- Catastrophic attack on the U.S. homeland or critical infrastructure;

- Threats or attacks against U.S. citizens abroad and our allies;

- Global economic crisis or widespread economic slowdown;

- Proliferation and/or use of weapons of mass destruction;

- Severe global infectious disease outbreaks;

- Climate change;

- Major energy market disruptions; and

- Significant security consequences associated with weak or failing states (including mass atrocities, regional spillover, and transnational organized crime).

We will seize strategic opportunities to shape the economic order and cultivate new relationships with emerging economic powers and countries newly committed to peaceful democratic change. We will also capitalize on the potential to end extreme poverty and build upon our comparative advantages in innovation, science and technology, entrepreneurship, and greater energy security.

We will **lead with strength.** After a difficult decade, America is growing stronger every day. The U.S. economy remains the most dynamic and resilient on Earth. We have rebounded from a global recession by creating more jobs in the United States than in all other advanced economies combined. Our military might is unrivaled. Yet, American exceptionalism is not rooted solely in the strength of our arms or economy. Above all, it is the product of our founding values, including the rule of law and universal rights, as well as the grit, talent, and diversity of the American people.

In the last 6 years alone, we arrested the worst financial crisis since the Great Depression and catalyzed a new era of economic growth. We increased our competitive edge and leadership in education, energy, science and technology, research and development, and healthcare. We achieved an energy transformation in North America. We are fortifying our critical infrastructure against all hazards, especially cyber espionage and attack. And we are working hard to safeguard our civil liberties while advancing our security.

America's strategic fundamentals are strong but should not be taken for granted. We must be innovative and judicious in how we use our resources to build up our national power. Going forward, we will strengthen our foundation by growing our economy, modernizing our defense, upholding our values, enhancing the resilience of our homeland, and promoting talent and diversity in our national security workforce.

We will **lead by example.** The strength of our institutions and our respect for the rule of law sets an example for democratic governance. When we uphold our values at home, we are better able to promote them in the world. This means safeguarding the civil rights and liberties of our citizens while increasing transparency and accountability. It also means holding ourselves to international norms and standards that we expect other nations to uphold, and admitting when we do not. We must also demonstrate our ability to forge diverse partnerships across our political spectrum. Many achievements of recent years were made possible by Democrats and Republicans; Federal, state and local governments; and the public and private sectors working together. But, we face continued challenges, including political dysfunction in Washington that undermines national unity, stifles bipartisan cooperation, and ultimately erodes the perception and strength of our leadership abroad. American leadership is always most powerful when we are able to forge common ground at home around key national priorities.

We will **lead with capable partners.** In an interconnected world, there are no global problems that can be solved without the United States, and few that can be solved by the United States alone. American leadership remains essential for mobilizing collective action to address global risks and seize strategic opportunities. Our closest partners and allies will remain the cornerstone of our international engagement. Yet, we will continuously expand the scope of cooperation to encompass other state partners, non-state and private actors, and international institutions—particularly the United Nations (U.N.), international financial institutions, and key regional organizations. These partnerships can deliver essential capacity to share the burdens of maintaining global security and prosperity and to uphold the norms that govern responsible international behavior. At the same time, we and our partners must make the reforms and investments needed to make sure we can work more effectively with each other while growing the ranks of responsible, capable states. The United States is safer and stronger when fewer people face destitution, when our trading partners are flourishing, and when societies are freer.

We will **lead with all the instruments of U.S. power.** Our influence is greatest when we combine all our strategic advantages. Our military will remain ready to defend our enduring national interests while providing essential leverage for our diplomacy. The use of force is not, however, the only tool at our disposal, and it is not the principal means of U.S. engagement abroad, nor always the most effective for the challenges we face. Rather, our first line of action is principled and clear-eyed diplomacy, combined with the central role of development in the forward defense and promotion of America's interests. We will continue pursuing measures to enhance the security of our diplomats and development professionals to ensure they can fulfill their responsibilities safely in high-risk environments. We will also leverage a strong and well-regulated economy to promote trade and investment while protecting the international financial system from abuse. Targeted economic sanctions will remain an effective tool for imposing costs on irresponsible actors and helping to dismantle criminal and terrorist networks. All our tools are made more effective by the skill of our intelligence professionals and the quality of intelligence they collect, analyze, and produce. Finally, we will apply our distinct advantages in law enforcement, science and technology, and people-to-people relationships to maximize the strategic effects of our national power.

We will **lead with a long-term perspective.** Around the world, there are historic transitions underway that will unfold over decades. This strategy positions America to influence their trajectories, seize the opportunities they create, and manage the risks they present. Five recent transitions, in particular, have significantly changed the security landscape, including since our last strategy in 2010.

First, power among states is more dynamic. The increasing use of the G-20 on global economic matters reflects an evolution in economic power, as does the rise of Asia, Latin America, and Africa. As the balance of economic power changes, so do expectations about influence over international affairs. Shifting power dynamics create both opportunities and risks for cooperation, as some states have been more willing than others to assume responsibilities commensurate with their greater economic capacity. In particular, India's potential, China's rise, and Russia's aggression all significantly impact the future of major power relations.

Second, power is shifting below and beyond the nation-state. Governments once able to operate with few checks and balances are increasingly expected to be more accountable to sub-state and non-state actors—from mayors of mega-cities and leaders in private industry to a more empowered civil society. They are also contending with citizens enabled by technology, youth as a majority in many societies, and a growing global middle class with higher expectations for governance and economic opportunity. While largely positive, these trends can foster violent non-state actors and foment instability—especially in fragile states where governance is weak or has broken down—or invite backlash by authoritarian regimes determined to preserve the power of the state.

Third, the increasing interdependence of the global economy and rapid pace of technological change are linking individuals, groups, and governments in unprecedented ways. This enables and incentivizes new forms of cooperation to establish dynamic security networks, expand international trade and investment, and transform global communications. It also creates shared vulnerabilities, as interconnected systems and sectors are susceptible to the threats of climate change, malicious cyber activity, pandemic diseases, and transnational terrorism and crime.

Fourth, a struggle for power is underway among and within many states of the Middle East and North Africa. This is a generational struggle in the aftermath of the 2003 Iraq war and 2011 Arab uprisings, which will redefine the region as well as relationships among communities and between citizens and their governments. This process will continue to be combustible, especially in societies where religious extremists take root, or rulers reject democratic reforms, exploit their economies, and crush civil society.

Fifth, the global energy market has changed dramatically. The United States is now the world's largest natural gas and oil producer. Our dependence on foreign oil is at a 20-year low—and declining—and we are leading a new clean energy economy. While production in the Middle East and elsewhere remains vitally important for the global market, increased U.S. production is helping keep markets well-supplied and prices conducive to economic growth. On the other hand, energy security concerns have been exacerbated by European dependence on Russian natural gas and the willingness of Russia to use energy for political ends. At the same time, developing countries now consume more energy than developed ones, which is altering energy flows and changing consumer relationships.

Today's strategic environment is fluid. Just as the United States helped shape the course of events in the last century, so must we influence their trajectory today by evolving the way we exercise American leadership. This strategy outlines priorities based on a realistic assessment of the risks to our enduring national interests and the opportunities for advancing them. This strategy eschews orienting our entire foreign policy around a single threat or region. It establishes instead a diversified and balanced set of priorities appropriate for the world's leading global power with interests in every part of an increasingly interconnected world.

II. Security

The United States government has no greater responsibility than protecting the American people. Yet, our obligations do not end at our borders. We embrace our responsibilities for underwriting international security because it serves our interests, upholds our commitments to allies and partners, and addresses threats that are truly global. There is no substitute for American leadership whether in the face of aggression, in the cause of universal values, or in the service of a more secure America. Fulfilling our responsibilities depends on a strong defense and secure homeland. It also requires a global security posture in which our unique capabilities are employed within diverse international coalitions and in support of local partners. Such a shift is possible after a period of prolonged combat. Six years ago, there were roughly 180,000 U.S. troops in Iraq and Afghanistan. Today, there are fewer than 15,000. This transition has dramatically reduced U.S. casualties and allows us to realign our forces and resources to meet an evolving set of threats while securing our strategic objectives.

In so doing, we will prioritize collective action to meet the persistent threat posed by terrorism today, especially from al-Qa'ida, ISIL, and their affiliates. In addition to acting decisively to defeat direct threats, we will focus on building the capacity of others to prevent the causes and consequences of conflict to include countering extreme and dangerous ideologies. Keeping nuclear materials from terrorists and preventing the proliferation of nuclear weapons remains a high priority, as does mobilizing the international community to meet the urgent challenges posed by climate change and infectious disease. Collective action is needed to assure access to the shared spaces—cyber, space, air, and oceans—where the dangerous behaviors of some threaten us all.

Our allies will remain central to all these efforts. The North Atlantic Treaty Organization (NATO) is the world's preeminent multilateral alliance, reinforced by the historic close ties we have with the United Kingdom, France, Germany, Italy, and Canada. NATO is stronger and more cohesive than at any point in its history, especially due to contributions of the Nordic countries and newer members like Poland and the Baltic countries. Our alliances in Asia underwrite security and enable prosperity throughout Asia and the Pacific. We will continue to modernize these essential bilateral alliances while enhancing the security ties among our allies. Japan, South Korea, and Australia, as well as our close partner in New Zealand, remain the model for interoperability while we reinvigorate our ties to the Philippines and preserve our ties to Thailand. And our allies and partners in other regions, including our security partnership and people-to-people ties with Israel, are essential to advancing our interests.

Strengthen Our National Defense

A strong military is the bedrock of our national security. During over a decade of war, the All Volunteer Force has answered our Nation's call. To maintain our military edge and readiness, we will continue to insist on reforms and necessary investment in our military forces and their families. Our military will remain ready to deter and defeat threats to the homeland, including against missile, cyber, and terrorist attacks, while mitigating the effects of potential attacks and natural disasters. Our military is postured globally to protect our citizens and interests, preserve regional stability, render humanitarian assistance and disaster relief, and build the capacity of our partners to join with us in meeting security challenges.

U.S. forces will continue to defend the homeland, conduct global counterterrorism operations, assure allies, and deter aggression through forward presence and engagement. If deterrence fails, U.S. forces will be ready to project power globally to defeat and deny aggression in multiple theaters.

As we modernize, we will apply the lessons of past drawdowns. Although our military will be smaller, it must remain dominant in every domain. With the Congress, we must end sequestration and enact critical reforms to build a versatile and responsive force prepared for a more diverse set of contingencies. We will protect our investment in foundational capabilities like the nuclear deterrent, and we will grow our investment in crucial capabilities like cyber; space; and intelligence, surveillance, and reconnaissance. We will safeguard our science and technology base to keep our edge in the capabilities needed to prevail against any adversary. Above all, we will take care of our people. We will recruit and retain the best talent while developing leaders committed to an ethical and expert profession of arms. We will honor our sacred trust with Veterans and the families and communities that support them, making sure those who have served have the benefits, education, and opportunities they have earned.

We will be principled and selective in the use of force. The use of force should not be our first choice, but it will sometimes be the necessary choice. The United States will use military force, unilaterally if necessary, when our enduring interests demand it: when our people are threatened; when our livelihoods are at stake; and when the security of our allies is in danger. In these circumstances, we prefer to act with allies and partners. The threshold for military action is higher when our interests are not directly threatened. In such cases, we will seek to mobilize allies and partners to share the burden and achieve lasting outcomes. In all cases, the decision to use force must reflect a clear mandate and feasible objectives, and we must ensure our actions are effective, just, and consistent with the rule of law. It should be based on a serious appreciation for the risk to our mission, our global responsibilities, and the opportunity costs at home and abroad. Whenever and wherever we use force, we will do so in a way that reflects our values and strengthens our legitimacy.

Reinforce Homeland Security

Our homeland is more secure. But, we must continue to learn and adapt to evolving threats and hazards. We are better able to guard against terrorism—the core responsibility of homeland security—as well as illicit networks and other threats and hazards due to improved information sharing, aviation and border security, and international cooperation. We have emphasized community-based efforts and local law enforcement programs to counter homegrown violent extremism and protect vulnerable individuals from extremist ideologies that could lead them to join conflicts overseas or carry out attacks here at home. Through risk-based approaches, we have countered terrorism and transnational organized crime in ways that enhance commerce, travel, and tourism and, most fundamentally, preserve our civil liberties. We are more responsive and resilient when prevention fails or disaster strikes as witnessed with the Boston Marathon bombings and Hurricane Sandy.

The essential services that underpin American society must remain secure and functioning in the face of diverse threats and hazards. Therefore, we take a Whole of Community approach, bringing together all elements of our society—individuals, local communities, the private and non-profit sectors, faith-based organizations, and all levels of government—to make sure America is resilient in the face of adversity.

We are working with the owners and operators of our Nation's critical cyber and physical infrastructure across every sector—financial, energy, transportation, health, information technology, and more—to decrease vulnerabilities and increase resilience. We are partnering with states and local communities to better plan for, absorb, recover from, and adapt to adverse events brought about by the compounding effects of climate change. We will also continue to enhance pandemic preparedness at home and address the threat arising from new drug-resistant microbes and biological agents.

Combat the Persistent Threat of Terrorism

The threat of catastrophic attacks against our homeland by terrorists has diminished but still persists. An array of terrorist threats has gained traction in areas of instability, limited opportunity, and broken governance. Our adversaries are not confined to a distinct country or region. Instead, they range from South Asia through the Middle East and into Africa. They include globally oriented groups like al-Qa'ida and its affiliates, as well as a growing number of regionally focused and globally connected groups—many with an al-Qa'ida pedigree like ISIL, which could pose a threat to the homeland.

We have drawn from the experience of the last decade and put in place substantial changes to our efforts to combat terrorism, while preserving and strengthening important tools that have been developed since 9/11. Specifically, we shifted away from a model of fighting costly, large-scale ground wars in Iraq and Afghanistan in which the United States—particularly our military—bore an enormous burden. Instead, we are now pursuing a more sustainable approach that prioritizes targeted counterterrorism operations, collective action with responsible partners, and increased efforts to prevent the growth of violent extremism and radicalization that drives increased threats. Our leadership will remain essential to disrupting the unprecedented flow of foreign terrorist fighters to and from conflict zones. We will work to address the underlying conditions that can help foster violent extremism such as poverty, inequality, and repression. This means supporting alternatives to extremist messaging and greater economic opportunities for women and disaffected youth. We will help build the capacity of the most vulnerable states and communities to defeat terrorists locally. Working with the Congress, we will train and equip local partners and provide operational support to gain ground against terrorist groups. This will include efforts to better fuse and share information and technology as well as to support more inclusive and accountable governance.

In all our efforts, we aim to draw a stark contrast between what we stand for and the heinous deeds of terrorists. We reject the lie that America and its allies are at war with Islam. We will continue to act lawfully. Outside of areas of active hostilities, we endeavor to detain, interrogate, and prosecute terrorists through law enforcement. However, when there is a continuing, imminent threat, and when capture or other actions to disrupt the threat are not feasible, we will not hesitate to take decisive action. We will always do so legally, discriminately, proportionally, and bound by strict accountability and strong oversight. The United States—not our adversaries—will define the nature and scope of this struggle, lest it define us.

Our counterterrorism approach is at work with several states, including Somalia, Afghanistan and Iraq. In Afghanistan, we have ended our combat mission and transitioned to a dramatically smaller force focused on the goal of a sovereign and stable partner in Afghanistan that is not a safe haven for international terrorists. This has been made possible by the extraordinary sacrifices of our U.S. military, civilians throughout the interagency, and our international partners. They delivered justice to Osama bin Laden and significantly degraded al-Qa'ida's core leadership. They helped increase life expectancy, access to education, and opportunities for women and girls. Going forward, we will work with partners to carry out a limited counterterrorism mission against the remnants of core al-Qa'ida and maintain our support to the Afghan National Security Forces (ANSF). We are working with NATO and our other partners to train, advise, and assist the ANSF as a new government takes responsibility for the security and well-being of Afghanistan's citizens. We will continue to help improve governance that expands opportunity for all Afghans, including women and girls. We will also work with the countries of the region, including Pakistan, to mitigate the threat from terrorism and to support a viable peace and reconciliation process to end the violence in Afghanistan and improve regional stability.

We have undertaken a comprehensive effort to degrade and ultimately defeat ISIL. We will continue to support Iraq as it seeks to free itself from sectarian conflict and the scourge of extremists. Our support is tied to the government's willingness to govern effectively and inclusively and to ensure ISIL cannot sustain a safe haven on Iraqi territory. This requires professional and accountable Iraqi Security Forces that can overcome sectarian divides and protect all Iraqi citizens. It also requires international support, which is why we are leading an unprecedented international coalition to work with the Iraqi government and strengthen its military to regain sovereignty. Joined by our allies and partners, including multiple countries in the region, we employed our unique military capabilities to arrest ISIL's advance and to degrade their capabilities in both Iraq and Syria. At the same time, we are working with our partners to train and equip a moderate Syrian opposition to provide a counterweight to the terrorists and the brutality of the Assad regime. Yet, the only lasting solution to Syria's civil war remains political—an inclusive political transition that responds to the legitimate aspirations of all Syrian citizens.

Build Capacity to Prevent Conflict

We will strengthen U.S. and international capacity to prevent conflict among and within states. In the realm of inter-state conflict, Russia's violation of Ukraine's sovereignty and territorial integrity—as well as its belligerent stance toward other neighboring countries—endangers international norms that have largely been taken for granted since the end of the Cold War. Meanwhile, North Korean provocation and tensions in the East and South China Seas are reminders of the risks of escalation. American diplomacy and leadership, backed by a strong military, remain essential to deterring future acts of inter-state aggression and provocation by reaffirming our security commitments to allies and partners, investing in their capabilities to withstand coercion, imposing costs on those who threaten their neighbors or violate fundamental international norms, and embedding our actions within wider regional strategies.

Within states, the nexus of weak governance and widespread grievance allows extremism to take root, violent non-state actors to rise up, and conflict to overtake state structures. To meet these challenges, we will continue to work with partners and through multilateral organizations to address the root causes of conflict before they erupt and to contain and resolve them when they do. We prefer to partner with those fragile states that have a genuine political commitment to establishing legitimate governance and providing for their people. The focus of our efforts will be on proven areas of need and impact, such as inclusive politics, enabling effective and equitable service delivery, reforming security and rule of law sectors, combating corruption and organized crime, and promoting economic opportunity, particularly among youth and women. We will continue to lead the effort to ensure women serve as mediators of conflict and in peacebuilding efforts, and they are protected from gender-based violence.

We will continue to bolster the capacity of the U.N. and regional organizations to help resolve disputes, build resilience to crises and shocks, strengthen governance, end extreme poverty, and increase prosperity, so that fragile states can provide for the basic needs of their citizens and can avoid being vulnerable hosts for extremism and terrorism. We will meet our financial commitments to the U.N., press for reforms to strengthen peacekeeping, and encourage more contributions from advanced militaries. We will strengthen the operational capacity of regional organizations like the African Union (AU) and broaden the ranks of capable troop-contributing countries, including through the African Peacekeeping Rapid Response Partnership, which will help African countries rapidly deploy to emerging crises.

Prevent the Spread and Use of Weapons of Mass Destruction

No threat poses as grave a danger to our security and well-being as the potential use of nuclear weapons and materials by irresponsible states or terrorists. We therefore seek the peace and security of a world without nuclear weapons. As long as nuclear weapons exist, the United States must invest the resources necessary to maintain—without testing—a safe, secure, and effective nuclear deterrent that preserves strategic stability. However, reducing the threat requires us to constantly reinforce the basic bargain of the Nuclear Non-Proliferation Treaty, which commits nuclear weapons states to reduce their stockpiles while non-nuclear weapons states remain committed to using nuclear energy only for peaceful purposes. For our part, we are reducing the role and number of nuclear weapons through New START and our own strategy. We will continue to push for the entry into force of important multilateral agreements like the Comprehensive Nuclear Test-Ban Treaty and the various regional nuclear weapons-free zone protocols, as well as the creation of a Fissile Material Cut-Off Treaty.

Vigilance is required to stop countries and non-state actors from developing or acquiring nuclear, chemical, or biological weapons, or the materials to build them. The Nuclear Security Summit process has catalyzed a global effort to lock down vulnerable nuclear materials and institutionalize nuclear security best practices. Our commitment to the denuclearization of the Korean Peninsula is rooted in the profound risks posed by North Korean weapons development and proliferation. Our efforts to remove and destroy chemical weapons in Libya and Syria reflect our leadership in implementation and progress toward universalization of the Chemical Weapons Convention.

We have made clear Iran must meet its international obligations and demonstrate its nuclear program is entirely peaceful. Our sanctions regime has demonstrated that the international community can—and will—hold accountable those nations that do not meet their obligations, while also opening up a space for a diplomatic resolution. Having reached a first step arrangement that stops the progress of Iran's nuclear program in exchange for limited relief, our preference is to achieve a comprehensive and verifiable deal that assures Iran's nuclear program is solely for peaceful purposes. This is the best way to advance our interests, strengthen the global nonproliferation regime, and enable Iran to access peaceful nuclear energy. However, we retain all options to achieve the objective of preventing Iran from producing a nuclear weapon.

Confront Climate Change

Climate change is an urgent and growing threat to our national security, contributing to increased natural disasters, refugee flows, and conflicts over basic resources like food and water. The present day effects of climate change are being felt from the Arctic to the Midwest. Increased sea levels and storm surges threaten coastal regions, infrastructure, and property. In turn, the global economy suffers, compounding the growing costs of preparing and restoring infrastructure.

America is leading efforts at home and with the international community to confront this challenge. Over the last 6 years, U.S. emissions have declined by a larger total magnitude than those of any other country. Through our Climate Action Plan and related executive actions, we will go further with a goal of reducing greenhouse gas emissions by 26 to 28 percent of 2005 levels by 2025. Working with U.S. states and private utilities, we will set the first-ever standards to cut the amount of carbon pollution our power plants emit into the air. We are also working to strengthen resilience and address vulnerabilities to climate impacts.

These domestic efforts contribute to our international leadership. Building on the progress made in Copenhagen and in ensuing negotiations, we are working toward an ambitious new global climate change agreement to shape standards for prevention, preparedness, and response over the next decade. As the world's two largest emitters, the United States and China reached a landmark agreement to take significant action to reduce carbon pollution. The substantial contribution we have pledged to the Green Climate Fund will help the most vulnerable developing nations deal with climate change, reduce their carbon pollution, and invest in clean energy. More than 100 countries have also joined with us to reduce greenhouse gases under the Montreal Protocol—the same agreement the world used successfully to phase out ozone-depleting chemicals. We are partnering with African entrepreneurs to launch clean energy projects and helping farmers practice climate-smart agriculture and plant more durable crops. We are also driving collective action to reduce methane emissions from pipelines and to launch a free trade agreement for environmental goods.

Assure Access to Shared Spaces

The world is connected by shared spaces—cyber, space, air, and oceans—that enable the free flow of people, goods, services, and ideas. They are the arteries of the global economy and civil society, and access is at risk due to increased competition and provocative behaviors. Therefore, we will continue to promote rules for responsible behavior while making sure we have the capabilities to assure access to these shared spaces.

Cybersecurity

As the birthplace of the Internet, the United States has a special responsibility to lead a networked world. Prosperity and security increasingly depend on an open, interoperable, secure, and reliable Internet. Our economy, safety, and health are linked through a networked infrastructure that is targeted by malicious government, criminal, and individual actors who try to avoid attribution. Drawing on the voluntary cybersecurity framework, we are securing Federal networks and working with the private sector, civil society, and other stakeholders to strengthen the security and resilience of U.S. critical infrastructure. We will continue to work with the Congress to pursue a legislative framework that ensures high standards. We will defend ourselves, consistent with U.S. and international law, against cyber attacks and impose costs on malicious cyber actors, including through prosecution of illegal cyber activity. We will assist other countries to develop laws that enable strong action against threats that originate from their infrastructure. Globally, cybersecurity requires that long-standing norms of international behavior—to include protection of intellectual property, online freedom, and respect for civilian infrastructure—be upheld, and the Internet be managed as a shared responsibility between states and the private sector with civil society and Internet users as key stakeholders.

Space Security

Space systems allow the world to navigate and communicate with confidence to save lives, conduct commerce, and better understand the human race, our planet, and the depths of the universe. As countries increasingly derive benefits from space, we must join together to deal with threats posed by those who may wish to deny the peaceful use of outer space. We are expanding our international space cooperation activities in all sectors, promoting transparency and confidence-building measures such as an International Code of Conduct on Outer Space Activities, and expanding partnerships with the private sector in support of missions and capabilities previously claimed by governments alone. We will also develop technologies and tactics to deter and defeat efforts to attack our space systems; enable indications, warning, and attributions of such attacks; and enhance the resiliency of critical U.S. space capabilities.

Air and Maritime Security

The United States has an enduring interest in freedom of navigation and overflight as well as the safety and sustainability of the air and maritime environments. We will therefore maintain the capability to ensure the free flow of commerce, to respond quickly to those in need, and to deter those who might contemplate aggression. We insist on safe and responsible behaviors in the sky and at sea. We reject illegal and aggressive claims to airspace and in the maritime domain and condemn deliberate attacks on commercial passenger traffic. On territorial disputes, particularly in Asia, we denounce coercion and assertive behaviors that threaten escalation. We encourage open channels of dialogue to resolve disputes peacefully in accordance with international law. We also support the early conclusion of an effective code of conduct for the South China Sea between China and the Association of Southeast Asian States (ASEAN). America's ability to press for the observance of established customary international law reflected in the U.N. Convention on the Law of the Sea will be enhanced if the Senate provides its advice and consent—the ongoing failure to ratify this Treaty undermines our national interest in a rules-based international order. Finally, we seek to build on the unprecedented international cooperation of the last few years, especially in the Arctic as well as in combatting piracy off the Horn of Africa and drug-smuggling in the Caribbean Sea and across Southeast Asia.

Increase Global Health Security

The spread of infectious diseases constitute a growing risk. The Ebola epidemic in West Africa high-lights the danger of a raging virus. The spread of new microbes or viruses, the rise and spread of drug resistance, and the deliberate release of pathogens all represent threats that are exacerbated by the globalization of travel, food production and supply, and medical products. Despite important scientific, technological, and organizational accomplishments, most countries have not yet achieved international core competencies for health security, and many lack sufficient capacity to prevent, detect, or respond to disease outbreaks.

America is the world leader in fighting pandemics, including HIV/AIDS, and in improving global health security. At home, we are strengthening our ability to prevent outbreaks and ensure sufficient capacity to respond rapidly and manage biological incidents. As an exemplar of a modern and responsive public health system, we will accelerate our work with partners through the Global Health Security Agenda in pursuit of a world that is safer and more secure from infectious disease. We will save lives by strengthening regulatory frameworks for food safety and developing a global system to prevent avoidable epidemics, detect and report disease outbreaks in real time, and respond more rapidly and effectively. Finally, we will continue to lead efforts to combat the rise of antibiotic resistant bacteria.

III. Prosperity

Our economy is the largest, most open, and innovative in the world. Our leadership has also helped usher in a new era of unparalleled global prosperity. Sustaining our leadership depends on shaping an emerging global economic order that continues to reflect our interests and values. Despite its success, our rules-based system is now competing against alternative, less-open models. Moreover, the American consumer cannot sustain global demand—growth must be more balanced. To meet this challenge, we must be strategic in the use of our economic strength to set new rules of the road, strengthen our partnerships, and promote inclusive development.

Through our trade and investment policies, we will shape globalization so that it is working for American workers. By leveraging our improved economic and energy position, we will strengthen the global financial system and advance high-standard trade deals. We will ensure tomorrow's global trading system is consistent with our interests and values by seeking to establish and enforce rules through international institutions and regional initiatives and by addressing emerging challenges like state-owned enterprises and digital protectionism. U.S. markets and educational opportunities will help the next generation of global entrepreneurs sustain momentum in growing a global middle class. To prevent conflict and promote human dignity, we will also pursue policies that eradicate extreme poverty and reduce inequality.

Put Our Economy to Work

The American economy is an engine for global economic growth and a source of stability for the international system. In addition to being a key measure of power and influence in its own right, it underwrites our military strength and diplomatic influence. A strong economy, combined with a prominent U.S. presence in the global financial system, creates opportunities to advance our security.

To ensure our economic competitiveness, we are investing in a new foundation for sustained economic growth that creates good jobs and rising incomes. Because knowledge is the currency of today's global economy, we must keep expanding access to early childhood and affordable higher education. The further acceleration of our manufacturing revolution will create the next generation of high technology manufacturing jobs. Immigration reform that combines smart and effective enforcement of the law with a pathway to citizenship for those who earn it remains an imperative. We will deliver quality, affordable healthcare to more and more Americans. We will also support job creation, strengthen the middle class, and spur economic growth by opening markets and leveling the playing field for American workers and businesses abroad. Jobs will also grow as we expand our work with trading partners to eliminate barriers to the full deployment of U.S. innovation in the digital space. These efforts are complemented by more modern and reliable infrastructure that ensures safety and enables growth.

In addition to the positive benefits of trade and commerce, a strong and well-regulated economy positions the United States to lead international efforts to promote financial transparency and prevent the global financial system from being abused by transnational criminal and terrorist organizations to engage in, or launder the proceeds of illegal activity. We will continue to work within the Financial Action Task Force, the G-20, and other fora to enlist all nations in the fight to protect the integrity of the global financial system.

Advance Our Energy Security

The United States is now the world leader in oil and gas production. America's energy revival is not only good for growth, it offers new buffers against the coercive use of energy by some and new opportunities for helping others transition to low-carbon economies. American oil production has increased dramatically, impacting global markets. Imports have decreased substantially, reducing the funds we send overseas. Consumption has declined, reducing our vulnerability to global supply disruption and price shocks. However, we still have a significant stake in the energy security of our allies in Europe and elsewhere. Seismic shifts in supply and demand are underway across the globe. Increasing global access to reliable and affordable energy is one of the most powerful ways to support social and economic development and to help build new markets for U.S. technology and investment.

The challenges faced by Ukrainian and European dependence on Russian energy supplies puts a spotlight on the need for an expanded view of energy security that recognizes the collective needs of the United States, our allies, and trading partners as well as the importance of competitive energy markets. Therefore, we must promote diversification of energy fuels, sources, and routes, as well as encourage indigenous sources of energy supply. Greater energy security and independence within the Americas is central to these efforts. We will also stay engaged with global suppliers and our partners to reduce the potential for energy-related conflict in places like the Arctic and Asia. Our energy security will be further enhanced by living up to commitments made in the Rome Declaration and through our all-of-the-above energy strategy for a low-carbon world. We will continue to develop American fossil resources while becoming a more efficient country that develops cleaner, alternative fuels and vehicles. We are demonstrating that America can and will lead the global economy while reducing our emissions.

Lead in Science, Technology, and Innovation

Scientific discovery and technological innovation empower American leadership with a competitive edge that secures our military advantage, propels our economy, and improves the human condition. Sustaining that edge requires robust Federal investments in basic and applied research. We must also strengthen science, technology, engineering, and mathematics (STEM) education to produce tomorrow's discoverers, inventors, entrepreneurs, and high-skills workforce. Our commitment remains strong to preparation and compensation for STEM teachers, broadband connectivity and high-tech educational tools for schools, programs that inspire and provide opportunities for girls and underrepresented minorities, and support for innovation in STEM teaching and inclusion in higher education. We will also keep our edge by opening our national labs to more commercial partnerships while tapping research and development in the private sector, including a wide range of start-ups and firms at the leading edge of America's innovation economy.

Shape the Global Economic Order

We have recovered from the global economic crisis, but much remains to be done to shape the emerging economic order to avoid future crises. We have responsibilities at home to continue to improve our banking practices and forge ahead with regulatory reform, even as we press others to align with our robust standards. In addition to securing our immediate economic interests, we must drive the inclusive economic growth that creates demand for American exports. We will protect the free movement of information and work to prevent the risky behavior that led to the recent crisis, while addressing resurgent economic forces, from state capitalism to market-distorting free-riding.

American leadership is central to strengthening global finance rules and making sure they are consistent and transparent. We will work through the G-20 to reinforce the core architecture of the international financial and economic system, including the World Trade Organization, to ensure it is positioned to foster both stability and growth. We remain committed to governance reforms for these same institutions, including the World Bank and the International Monetary Fund, to make them more effective and representative. In so doing, we seek to ensure institutions reinforce, rather than undermine, an effective global financial system.

We believe trade agreements have economic and strategic benefits for the United States. We will therefore work with the Congress to achieve bipartisan renewal of Trade Promotion Authority and to advance a trade agenda that brings jobs to our shores, increases standards of living, strengthens our partners and allies, and promotes stability in critical regions. The United States has one of the most open economies in the world. Our tariffs are low, and we do not use regulation to discriminate against foreign goods. The same is not true throughout the world, which is why our trade agenda is focused on lowering tariffs on American products, breaking down barriers to our goods and services, and setting higher standards to level the playing field for American workers and firms.

Through the Trans-Pacific Partnership (TPP) and Transatlantic Trade and Investment Partnership (T-TIP), we are setting the world's highest standards for labor rights and environmental protection, while removing barriers to U.S. exports and putting the United States at the center of a free trade zone covering two-thirds of the global economy. Our goal is to use this position, along with our highly skilled workforce, strong rule of law, and abundant supply of affordable energy, to make America the production platform of choice and the premier investment destination. In addition to these major regional agreements, we will work to achieve groundbreaking agreements to liberalize trade in services, information technology, and environmental goods—areas where the United States is a global leader in innovation. And we will make it easier for businesses of all sizes to expand their reach by improving supply chains and regulatory cooperation.

All countries will benefit when we open markets further, extend and enhance tools such as the African Growth and Opportunity Act (AGOA), and reduce inefficiencies in the global trading system through trade facilitation improvements. And through our development initiatives—such as Power Africa, Trade Africa, Feed the Future, and the Open Government Partnership—we will continue to work closely with governments, the private sector, and civil society to foster inclusive economic growth, reduce corruption, and build capacity at the local level. Investment in critical infrastructure and security will facilitate trade among countries, especially for developing and emerging economies.

End Extreme Poverty

We have an historic opportunity to end extreme poverty within a generation and put our societies on a path of shared and sustained prosperity. In so doing, we will foster export markets for U.S. businesses, improve investment opportunities, and decrease the need for costly military interventions. Growth in the global economy has lifted hundreds of millions out of extreme poverty. We have already made significant progress guided in part through global consensus and mobilization around the Millennium Development Goals. The world cut the percentage of people living in extreme poverty in half between 1990 and 2010. In that period, nearly 800 million people rose above the international poverty line. By 2012, child deaths were down almost 50 percent since 1990. Twenty-nine countries registered as low-income in 2000 have today achieved middle-income status, and private capital and domestic resources far outstrip donor assistance as the primary means for financing development. Trends in economic growth also signal what is possible; sub-Saharan Africa has averaged an aggregate annual growth rate of over 5 percent for the last decade despite the disruptions of the world financial crisis.

We are now working with many partners to put ending extreme poverty at the center of a new global sustainable development agenda that will mobilize action for the next 15 years. We will press for transformative investments in areas like women's equality and empowerment, education, sustainable energy, and governance. We will use trade and investment to harness job-rich economic growth. We will concentrate on the clear need for country ownership and political commitment and reinforce the linkage between social and economic development. We will lead the effort to marshal diverse resources and broad coalitions to advance the imperative of accountable, democratic governance.

We will use our leadership to promote a model of financing that leverages billions in investment from the private sector and draws on America's scientific, technological, and entrepreneurial strengths to take to scale proven solutions in partnership with governments, business, and civil society. And we will leverage our leadership in promoting food security, enhancing resilience, modernizing rural agriculture, reducing the vulnerability of the poor, and eliminating preventable child and maternal deaths as we drive progress toward an AIDS-free generation.

IV. Values

To lead effectively in a world experiencing significant political change, the United States must live our values at home while promoting universal values abroad. From the Middle East to Ukraine to Southeast Asia to the Americas, citizens are more empowered in seeking greater freedoms and accountable institutions. But these demands have often produced an equal and opposite reaction from backers of discredited authoritarian orders, resulting in crackdowns and conflict. Many of the threats to our security in recent years arose from efforts by authoritarian states to oppose democratic forces—from the crisis caused by Russian aggression in Ukraine to the rise of ISIL within the Syrian civil war. By the same token, many of our greatest opportunities stem from advances for liberty and rule of law—from sub-Saharan Africa to Eastern Europe to Burma.

Defending democracy and human rights is related to every enduring national interest. It aligns us with the aspirations of ordinary people throughout the world. We know from our own history people must lead their own struggles for freedom if those struggles are to succeed. But America is also uniquely situated—and routinely expected—to support peaceful democratic change. We will continue mobilizing international support to strengthen and expand global norms of human rights. We will support women, youth, civil society, journalists, and entrepreneurs as drivers of change. We will continue to insist that governments uphold their human rights obligations, speak out against repression wherever it occurs, and work to prevent, and, if necessary, respond to mass atrocities.

Our closest allies in these efforts will be, as they always have, other democratic states. But, even where our strategic interests require us to engage governments that do not share all our values, we will continue to speak out clearly for human rights and human dignity in our public and private diplomacy. Any support we might provide will be balanced with an awareness of the costs of repressive policies for our own security interests and the democratic values by which we live. Because our human rights advocacy will be most effective when we work in concert with a wide range of partners, we are building coalitions with civil society, religious leaders, businesses, other governments, and international organizations. We will also work to ensure people enjoy the same rights—and security—online as they are entitled to enjoy offline by opposing efforts to restrict information and punish speech.

Live Our Values

Our values are a source of strength and security, and our ability to promote our values abroad is directly tied to our willingness to abide by them at home. In recent years, questions about America's post-9/11 security policies have often been exploited by our adversaries, while testing our commitment to civil liberties and the rule of law at home. For the sake of our security and our leadership in the world, it is essential we hold ourselves to the highest possible standard, even as we do what is necessary to secure our people.

To that end, we strengthened our commitment against torture and have prohibited so-called enhanced interrogation techniques that were contrary to American values, while implementing stronger safeguards for the humane treatment of detainees. We have transferred many detainees from Guantanamo Bay, and we are working with the Congress to remove the remaining restrictions on detainee transfers so that we can finally close it. Where prosecution is an option, we will bring terrorists to justice through both civilian and, when appropriate, reformed military commission proceedings that incorporate fundamental due process and other protections essential to the effective administration of justice.

Our vital intelligence activities are also being reformed to preserve the capabilities needed to secure our interests while continuing to respect privacy and curb the potential for abuse. We are increasing transparency so the public can be confident our surveillance activities are consistent with the rule of law and governed by effective oversight. We have not and will not collect signals intelligence to suppress criticism or dissent or to afford a competitive advantage to U.S. companies. Safeguards currently in place governing how we retain and share intelligence are being extended to protect personal information regardless of nationality.

Advance Equality

American values are reflective of the universal values we champion all around the world—including the freedoms of speech, worship, and peaceful assembly; the ability to choose leaders democratically; and the right to due process and equal administration of justice. We will be a champion for communities that are too frequently vulnerable to violence, abuse, and neglect—such as ethnic and religious minorities; people with disabilities; Lesbian, Gay, Bisexual, and Transgender (LGBT) individuals; displaced persons; and migrant workers.

Recognizing that no society will succeed if it does not draw on the potential of all its people, we are pressing for the political and economic participation of women and girls—who are too often denied their inalienable rights and face substantial barriers to opportunity in too many places. Our efforts include helping girls everywhere get the education they need to participate fully in the economy and realize their potential. We are focused on reducing the scourge of violence against women around the globe by providing support for affected populations and enhancing efforts to improve judicial systems so perpetrators are held accountable.

Support Emerging Democracies

The United States will concentrate attention and resources to help countries consolidate their gains and move toward more democratic and representative systems of governance. Our focus is on supporting countries that are moving in the right direction—whether it is the peaceful transitions of power we see in sub-Saharan Africa; the movement toward constitutional democracy in Tunisia; or the opening taking place in Burma. In each instance, we are creating incentives for positive reform and disincentives for backsliding.

The road from demanding rights in the square to building institutions that guarantee them is long and hard. In the last quarter century, parts of Eastern Europe, Latin America, Africa, and East Asia have consolidated transitions to democracy, but not without setbacks. The popular uprisings that began in the Arab world took place in a region with weaker democratic traditions, powerful authoritarian elites, sectarian tensions, and active violent extremist elements, so it is not surprising setbacks have thus far outnumbered triumphs. Yet, change is inevitable in the Middle East and North Africa, as it is in all places where the illusion of stability is artificially maintained by silencing dissent.

But the direction of that change is not predetermined. We will therefore continue to look for ways to support the success and ease the difficulties of democratic transitions through responsible assistance, investment and trade, and by supporting political, economic, and security reforms. We will continue to push for reforms in authoritarian countries not currently undergoing wholesale transitions. Good governance is also predicated on strengthening the state-society relationship. When citizens have a voice in the decisionmaking that affects them, governments make better decisions and citizens are better able to participate, innovate, and contribute.

The corrosive effects of corruption must be overcome. While information sharing allows us to identify corrupt officials more easily, globalization has also made it easier for corrupt officials to hide the proceeds of corruption abroad, increasing the need for strong and consistent implementation of the international standards on combating illicit finance. The United States is leading the way in promoting adherence to standards of accountable and transparent governance, including through initiatives like the Open Government Partnership. We will utilize a broad range of tools to recover assets stolen by corrupt officials and make it harder for criminals to hide, launder, and benefit from illegal proceeds. Our leadership toward governance that is more open, responsible, and accountable makes clear that democracy can deliver better government and development for ordinary people.

Empower Civil Society and Young Leaders

Democracy depends on more than elections, or even government institutions. Through civil society, citizens come together to hold their leaders accountable and address challenges. Civil society organizations often drive innovations and develop new ideas and approaches to solve social, economic, and political problems that governments can apply on a larger scale. Moreover, by giving people peaceful avenues to advance their interests and express their convictions, a free and flourishing civil society contributes to stability and helps to counter violent extremism.

Still, civil society and individual activists face challenges in many parts of the world. As technology empowers individuals and nongovernmental groups to mobilize around a wide array of issues—from countering corruption and advancing the rule of law to environmental activism—political elites in authoritarian states, and even in some with more democratic traditions, are acting to restrict space for civil society. Restrictions are often seen through new laws and regulations that deny groups the foreign funding they depend on to operate, that criminalize groups of people like the LGBT community, or deny political opposition groups the freedom to assemble in peaceful protest. The United States is countering this trend by providing direct support for civil society and by advocating rollback of laws and regulations that undermine citizens' rights. We are also supporting technologies that expand access to information, enable freedom of expression, and connect civil society groups in this fight around the world.

More than 50 percent of the world's people are under 30 years old. Many struggle to make a life in countries with broken governance. We are taking the initiative to build relationships with the world's young people, identifying future leaders in government, business, and civil society and connecting them to one another and to the skills they need to thrive. We have established new programs of exchange among young Americans and young people from Africa to Southeast Asia, building off the successes of the International Visitor and Young African Leaders initiatives. We are fostering increased education exchanges in our hemisphere. And we are catalyzing economic growth and innovation within societies by lifting up and promoting entrepreneurship.

Prevent Mass Atrocities

The mass killing of civilians is an affront to our common humanity and a threat to our common security. It destabilizes countries and regions, pushes refugees across borders, and creates grievances that extremists exploit. We have a strong interest in leading an international response to genocide and mass atrocities when they arise, recognizing options are more extensive and less costly when we act preventively before situations reach crisis proportions. We know the risk of mass atrocities escalates when citizens are denied basic rights and freedoms, are unable to hold accountable the institutions of government, or face unrelenting poverty and conflict. We affirm our support for the international consensus that governments have the responsibility to protect civilians from mass atrocities and that this responsibility passes to the broader international community when those governments manifestly fail to protect their populations. We will work with the international community to prevent and call to account those responsible for the worst human rights abuses, including through support to the International Criminal Court, consistent with U.S. law and our commitment to protecting our personnel. Moreover, we will continue to mobilize allies and partners to strengthen our collective efforts to prevent and respond to mass atrocities using all our instruments of national power.

V. International Order

We have an opportunity—and obligation—to lead the way in reinforcing, shaping, and where appropriate, creating the rules, norms, and institutions that are the foundation for peace, security, prosperity, and the protection of human rights in the 21st century. The modern-day international system currently relies heavily on an international legal architecture, economic and political institutions, as well as alliances and partnerships the United States and other like-minded nations established after World War II. Sustained by robust American leadership, this system has served us well for 70 years, facilitating international cooperation, burden sharing, and accountability. It carried us through the Cold War and ushered in a wave of democratization. It reduced barriers to trade, expanded free markets, and enabled advances in human dignity and prosperity.

But, the system has never been perfect, and aspects of it are increasingly challenged. We have seen too many cases where a failure to marshal the will and resources for collective action has led to inaction. The U.N. and other multilateral institutions are stressed by, among other things, resource demands, competing imperatives among member states, and the need for reform across a range of policy and administrative areas. Despite these undeniable strains, the vast majority of states do not want to replace the system we have. Rather, they look to America for the leadership needed to both fortify it and help it evolve to meet the wide range of challenges described throughout this strategy.

The United States will continue to make the development of sustainable solutions in all of these areas a foreign policy priority and devote diplomatic and other resources accordingly. We will continue to embrace the post-World War II legal architecture—from the U.N. Charter to the multilateral treaties that govern the conduct of war, respect for human rights, nonproliferation, and many other topics of global concern—as essential to the ordering of a just and peaceful world, where nations live peacefully within their borders, and all men and women have the opportunity to reach their potential. We will lead by example in fulfilling our responsibilities within this architecture, demonstrating to the world it is possible to protect security consistent with robust values. We will work vigorously both within the U.N. and other multilateral institutions, and with member states, to strengthen and modernize capacities—from peacekeeping to humanitarian relief—so they endure to provide protection, stability, and support for future generations.

At the same time, we will exact an appropriate cost on transgressors. Targeted economic sanctions remain an effective tool for imposing costs on those irresponsible actors whose military aggression, illicit proliferation, or unprovoked violence threaten both international rules and norms and the peace they were designed to preserve. We will pursue multilateral sanctions, including through the U.N., whenever possible, but will act alone, if necessary. Our sanctions will continue to be carefully designed and tailored to achieve clear aims while minimizing any unintended consequences for other economic actors, the global economy, and civilian populations.

In many cases, our use of targeted sanctions and other coercive measures are meant not only to uphold international norms, but to deter severe threats to stability and order at the regional level. We are not allowing the transgressors to define our regional strategies on the basis of the immediate threats they present. Rather, we are advancing a longer-term affirmative agenda in each of the regions, which prioritizes reinvigorating alliances with long-standing friends, making investments in new partnerships with emerging democratic powers with whom our interests are increasingly aligned, and continuing to support the development of capable, inclusive regional institutions to help enforce common international rules.

Advance Our Rebalance to Asia and the Pacific

The United States has been and will remain a Pacific power. Over the next 5 years, nearly half of all growth outside the United States is expected to come from Asia. That said, the security dynamics of the region—including contested maritime territorial claims and a provocative North Korea—risk escalation and conflict. American leadership will remain essential to shaping the region's long-term trajectory to enhance stability and security, facilitate trade and commerce through an open and transparent system, and ensure respect for universal rights and freedoms.

To realize this vision, we are diversifying our security relationships in Asia as well as our defense posture and presence. We are modernizing our alliances with Japan, South Korea, Australia, and the Philippines and enhancing the interactions among them to ensure they are fully capable of responding to regional and global challenges. We are committed to strengthening regional institutions such as ASEAN, the East Asia Summit, and Asia-Pacific Economic Cooperation to reinforce shared rules and norms, forge collective responses to shared challenges, and help ensure peaceful resolution of disputes. We are also working with our Asian partners to promote more open and transparent economies and regional support for international economic norms that are vital to maintaining it as an engine for global economic growth. The TPP is central to this effort.

As we have done since World War II, the United States will continue to support the advance of security, development, and democracy in Asia and the Pacific. This is an important focus of the deepening partnerships we are building in Southeast Asia including with Vietnam, Indonesia, and Malaysia. We will uphold our treaty obligations to Australia, South Korea, Japan, the Philippines, and Thailand, while encouraging the latter to return quickly to democracy. We will support the people of Burma to deepen and sustain reforms, including democratic consolidation and national reconciliation.

The United States welcomes the rise of a stable, peaceful, and prosperous China. We seek to develop a constructive relationship with China that delivers benefits for our two peoples and promotes security and prosperity in Asia and around the world. We seek cooperation on shared regional and global challenges such as climate change, public health, economic growth, and the denuclearization of the Korean Peninsula. While there will be competition, we reject the inevitability of confrontation. At the same time, we will manage competition from a position of strength while insisting that China uphold international rules and norms on issues ranging from maritime security to trade and human rights. We will closely monitor China's military modernization and expanding presence in Asia, while seeking ways to reduce the risk of misunderstanding or miscalculation. On cybersecurity, we will take necessary actions to protect our businesses and defend our networks against cyber-theft of trade secrets for commercial gain whether by private actors or the Chinese government.

In South Asia, we continue to strengthen our strategic and economic partnership with India. As the world's largest democracies, we share inherent values and mutual interests that form the cornerstone of our cooperation, particularly in the areas of security, energy, and the environment. We support India's role as a regional provider of security and its expanded participation in critical regional institutions. We see a strategic convergence with India's Act East policy and our continued implementation of the rebalance to Asia and the Pacific. At the same time, we will continue to work with both India and Pakistan to promote strategic stability, combat terrorism, and advance regional economic integration in South and Central Asia.

Strengthen Our Enduring Alliance with Europe

The United States maintains a profound commitment to a Europe that is free, whole, and at peace. A strong Europe is our indispensable partner, including for tackling global security challenges, promoting prosperity, and upholding international norms. Our work with Europe leverages our strong and historic bilateral relationships throughout the continent. We will steadfastly support the aspirations of countries in the Balkans and Eastern Europe toward European and Euro-Atlantic integration, continue to transform our relationship with Turkey, and enhance ties with countries in the Caucasus while encouraging resolution of regional conflict.

NATO is the strongest alliance the world has ever known and is the hub of an expanding global security network. Our Article 5 commitment to the collective defense of all NATO Members is ironclad, as is our commitment to ensuring the Alliance remains ready and capable for crisis response and cooperative security. We will continue to deepen our relationship with the European Union (EU), which has helped to promote peace and prosperity across the region, and deepen NATO-EU ties to enhance transatlantic security. To build on the millions of jobs supported by transatlantic trade, we support a pro-growth agenda in Europe to strengthen and broaden the region's recovery, and we seek an ambitious T-TIP to boost exports, support jobs, and raise global standards for trade.

Russia's aggression in Ukraine makes clear that European security and the international rules and norms against territorial aggression cannot be taken for granted. In response, we have led an international effort to support the Ukrainian people as they choose their own future and develop their democracy and economy. We are reassuring our allies by backing our security commitments and increasing responsiveness through training and exercises, as well as a dynamic presence in Central and Eastern Europe to deter further Russian aggression. This will include working with Europe to improve its energy security in both the short and long term. We will support partners such as Georgia, Moldova, and Ukraine so they can better work alongside the United States and NATO, as well as provide for their own defense.

And we will continue to impose significant costs on Russia through sanctions and other means while countering Moscow's deceptive propaganda with the unvarnished truth. We will deter Russian aggression, remain alert to its strategic capabilities, and help our allies and partners resist Russian coercion over the long term, if necessary. At the same time, we will keep the door open to greater collaboration with Russia in areas of common interests, should it choose a different path—a path of peaceful cooperation that respects the sovereignty and democratic development of neighboring states.

Seek Stability and Peace in the Middle East and North Africa

In the Middle East, we will dismantle terrorist networks that threaten our people, confront external aggression against our allies and partners, ensure the free flow of energy from the region to the world, and prevent the development, proliferation, or use of weapons of mass destruction. At the same time, we remain committed to a vision of the Middle East that is peaceful and prosperous, where democracy takes root and human rights are upheld. Sadly, this is not the case today, and nowhere is the violence more tragic and destabilizing than in the sectarian conflict from Beirut to Baghdad, which has given rise to new terrorist groups such as ISIL.

Resolving these connected conflicts, and enabling long-term stability in the region, requires more than the use and presence of American military forces. For one, it requires partners who can defend themselves. We are therefore investing in the ability of Israel, Jordan, and our Gulf partners to deter aggression while maintaining our unwavering commitment to Israel's security, including its Qualitative Military Edge. We are working with the Iraqi government to resolve Sunni grievances through more inclusive and responsive governance. With our partners in the region and around the world, we are leading a comprehensive counterterrorism strategy to degrade and ultimately defeat ISIL. At the same time, we will continue to pursue a lasting political solution to the devastating conflict in Syria.

Stability and peace in the Middle East and North Africa also requires reducing the underlying causes of conflict. America will therefore continue to work with allies and partners toward a comprehensive agreement with Iran that resolves the world's concerns with the Iranian nuclear program. We remain committed to ending the Israeli-Palestinian conflict through a two-state solution that ensures Israel's security and Palestine's viability. We will support efforts to deescalate sectarian tensions and violence between Shi'a and Sunni communities throughout the region. We will help countries in transition make political and economic reforms and build state capacity to maintain security, law and order, and respect for universal rights. In this respect, we seek a stable Yemen that undertakes difficult structural reforms and confronts an active threat from al-Qa'ida and other rebels. We will work with Tunisia to further progress on building democratic institutions and strengthening its economy. We will work with the U.N. and our Arab and European partners in an effort to help stabilize Libya and reduce the threat posed by lawless militias and extremists. And we will maintain strategic cooperation with Egypt to enable it to respond to shared security threats, while broadening our partnership and encouraging progress toward restoration of democratic institutions.

Invest in Africa's Future

Africa is rising. Many countries in Africa are making steady progress in growing their economies, improving democratic governance and rule of law, and supporting human rights and basic freedoms. Urbanization and a burgeoning youth population are changing the region's demographics, and young people are increasingly making their voices heard. But there are still many countries where the transition to democracy is uneven and slow with some leaders clinging to power. Corruption is endemic and public health systems are broken in too many places. And too many governments are responding to the expansion of civil society and free press by passing laws and adopting policies that erode that progress. Ongoing conflicts in Sudan, South Sudan, the Democratic Republic of the Congo, and the Central African

Republic, as well as violent extremists fighting governments in Somalia, Nigeria, and across the Sahel all pose threats to innocent civilians, regional stability, and our national security.

For decades, American engagement with Africa was defined by aid to help Africans reduce insecurity, famine, and disease. In contrast, the partnerships we are forging today, and will expand in the coming years, aim to build upon the aspirations of Africans. Through our Power Africa Initiative, we aim to double access to power in sub-Saharan Africa. We will increase trade and business ties, generating export-driven growth through initiatives like Trade Africa and AGOA. We will continue to support U.S. companies to deepen investment in what can be the world's next major center of global growth, including through the Doing Business in Africa campaign. Moreover, we are investing in tomorrow's leaders—the young entrepreneurs, innovators, civic leaders, and public servants who will shape the continent's future. We are strengthening civilian and military institutions through our Security Governance Initiative, and working to advance human rights and eliminate corruption. We are deepening our security partnerships with African countries and institutions, exemplified by our partnerships with the U.N. and AU in Mali and Somalia. Such efforts will help to resolve conflicts, strengthen African peacekeeping capacity, and counter transnational security threats while respecting human rights and the rule of law.

Our investment in nutrition and agricultural capacity will continue, reducing hunger through initiatives such as Feed the Future. We will keep working with partners to reduce deaths from Ebola, HIV/AIDS, malaria, and tuberculosis across Africa through such initiatives as the President's Emergency Plan for AIDS Relief and the Global Health Security Agenda. The Ebola epidemic in 2014 serves as a stark reminder of the threat posed by infectious disease and the imperative of global collective action to meet it. American leadership has proven essential to bringing to bear the international community to contain recent crises while building public health capacity to prevent future ones.

Deepen Economic and Security Cooperation in the Americas

We will continue to advance a Western Hemisphere that is prosperous, secure, democratic, and plays a greater global role. In the region as a whole, the number of people in the middle class has surpassed the number of people living in poverty for the first time in history, and the hemisphere is increasingly important to global energy supplies. These gains, however, are put at risk by weak institutions, high crime rates, powerful organized crime groups, an illicit drug trade, lingering economic disparity, and inadequate education and health systems.

To meet these challenges, we are working with Canada and Mexico to enhance our collective economic competitiveness while advancing prosperity in our hemisphere. With Chile, Peru, Mexico, and Canada, we are setting new global trade standards as we grow a strong contingent of countries in the Americas that favor open trading systems to include TPP. We seek to advance our economic partnership with Brazil, as it works to preserve gains in reducing poverty and deliver the higher standards of public services expected by the middle class.

We are also championing a strong and effective inter-American human rights and rule of law system. We are expanding our collaboration across the Americas to support democratic consolidation and increase public-private partnerships in education, sustainable development, access to electricity, climate resilience, and countering transnational organized crime.

Such collaboration is especially important in vulnerable countries like Guatemala, El Salvador, and Honduras, where government institutions are threatened by criminal syndicates. Migration surges involving unaccompanied children across our southern border is one major consequence of weak institutions and violence. American leadership, in partnership with these countries and with the support of their neighbors, remains essential to arresting the slide backwards and to creating steady improvements in economic growth and democratic governance. Likewise, we remain committed to helping rebuild Haiti and to put it and our other Caribbean neighbors on a path to sustainable development.

We will support the resolution of longstanding regional conflicts, particularly Colombia's conclusion of a peace accord with the Revolutionary Armed Forces of Colombia. Overall, we have deepened our strategic partnership with Colombia, which is a key contributor to international peace and security. Equally, we stand by the citizens of countries where the full exercise of democracy is at risk, such as Venezuela. Though a few countries in the region remain trapped in old ideological debates, we will keep working with all governments that are interested in cooperating with us in practical ways to reinforce the principles enumerated in the Inter-American Democratic Charter. As part of our effort to promote a fully democratic hemisphere, we will advance our new opening to Cuba in a way that most effectively promotes the ability of the Cuban people to determine their future freely.

VI. Conclusion

This *National Security Strategy* provides a vision for strengthening and sustaining American leadership in this still young century. It clarifies the purpose and promise of American power. It aims to advance our interests and values with initiative and from a position of strength. We will deter and defeat any adversary that threatens our national security and that of our allies. We confidently welcome the peaceful rise of other countries as partners to share the burdens for maintaining a more peaceful and prosperous world. We will continue to collaborate with established and emerging powers to promote our shared security and defend our common humanity, even as we compete with them in economic and other realms. We will uphold and refresh the international rules and norms that set the parameters for such collaboration and competition. We will do all of this and more with confidence that the international system whose creation we led in the aftermath of World War II will continue to serve America and the world well. This is an ambitious, but achievable agenda, especially if we continue to restore the bipartisan center that has been a pillar of strength for American foreign policy in decades past. America has greater capacity to adapt and recover from setbacks than any other country. A core element of our strength is our unity and our certainty that American leadership in this century, like the last, remains indispensable.

www.ingramcontent.com/pod-product-compliance
Lightning Source LLC
Chambersburg PA
CBHW080746290526
45790CB00008B/3346